The
Story
That Must Be
Told

Kimberly M. Wallace

PAGE PUBLISHING, INC.
Conneaut Lake, PA

First originally published by Page Publishing 2020

ISBN 978-1-64350-246-5 (pbk)
ISBN 978-1-64350-247-2 (digital)

Printed in the United States of America

Contents

Introduction

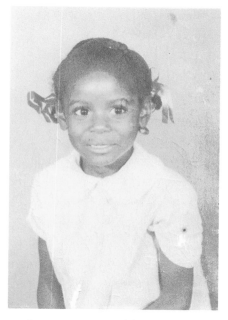

I was born in the mid to late 60's in the city of St. Louis Mo. at the Homer G. Phillips Hospital to (2) wonderful God fearing parents. I was the ninth child of (12) and was always told by my parents how much of a loving affectionate child I was and how I was always going from mom to dad kissing, hugging, and hanging onto them as early as (1) year old. I began walking at the fragile age of (9) months. At the tender age of 4ish I was violated by someone outside of my home and I would not come to share this information with my parents, siblings, anyone for that matter until the early 90's. This violation would prove to have had a terrible impact throughout my life. As a young girl, I enjoyed attending Sunday school, Sunday morning service, and Baptist Training Union everything involving church as we knew it. Every summer we had Vacation Bible school at our church and I couldn't wait until public school was over because I knew that in less than (2) weeks I would meet new people and would have fun learning about God and Jesus as my Savior. My siblings and I were the first ones at church because our mother was over the program. We as a family was apart of everything in the church because my mother was a missionary and my father the music professor and Church Trustee. At the age of (9) I was baptized by my uncle my mother's eldest brother whom was my pastor for (30) years until his passing in (2002). I looked forward to traveling every summer to our family reunions with my immediate and extended family. I also looked forward to the in and out of town trips with my church family. It would be remised of me if I didn't boast to you or maybe for a better choice of words express how exuberant I felt year after year coming in first place in the district and state convention's bible sword drills. This exercise depicts who could locate a specific scripture in the Bible at the allotted time and I would always beat the time. Yes my smile was a toothpaste moment. I was an usher for a while and I sung in the youth and adult choir for many years until I realized that God didn't call me to only praise Him in song because of my story, He wants me to tell the world my story.

Trust in the Lord with *all* of your heart lean not
to your own understanding; in *all* of your ways
acknowledge Him, and He will direct your path.
—Proverbs 3:5–6

This is not just something said for I know this to be the truth. Regardless of how I thought, I knew enough, and that I was strong enough to fight Satan in my own physical might which is going to die someday. I quickly remembered, "Without the power of Jesus there is nothing that I can do."

Now, as I look back at my introduction, and *all* that I have endured throughout the years expressed in this book, I say, "Thank you God, for you have brought me to this point and allows my readers, both broken and mended alike, to hold on to their faith and walk in victory to their destiny."

You can make it. You see, I chose to, and I am praying for your breakthrough, in Jesus name, amen.

The Beginning

On Thursday, May 13, 2004, the worst thing that I could've never imagined happened—my son, Charles Montez, was murdered. Charles was seventeen-years-old with a bright future as a basketball star. Charles was known to his family as "Chucky," but to his school family and those who were privileged to play basketball with him as "Showtime" (number 22). He was loved by so many people. On that afternoon, Charles had come home from school and asked me before sitting his bookbag on the bench in the foyer if he could go on the city's west side with his brother, cousin, and classmates. I, without hesitation, said, "No!"

Charles being as charming as he was known to be, kept asking me.

Finally, I looked him in his eyes and said, "Okay, you can go."

I can still see him with that big smile running to his brother's car so that he wouldn't get left. They had not been gone all of thirty minutes when I got a knock at my door from one of his classmates, who was also one of his closest friends. When I opened the door, he said, "Ms. Wallace, some people were shooting, and Charles got caught in the crossfire."

All I remember was slamming my front door, screaming for my husband to come downstairs and saying, "Go find my baby."

I picked up the phone that sat on the table in the foyer and dialed 911. When the operator answered, I said, "Some people were shooting and that my son got caught in the crossfire."

I wasn't making any sense at all. I couldn't even remember what street he was on, but I was begging them to find my son. I can't remember who it was, but as I hung up the phone someone came into my house and said that it was my nephew who was shot, not Chucky. I can admit I felt a little relieved but had begun hurting for my sister, the mother of my nephew.

Before I could fully settle in my train of thoughts, my mother walked in my house and said to me, "Kim, Chucky has been shot, and he needs you."

Oh God, those words still pierce my soul today as I sit here writing with tears flowing down my face. It was my dad, my husband, and me that got in the car and drove to Barnes Hospital. It was a beautiful sunny day, and all of a sudden, as we're making this seven-minute ride, it began to pour down raining. As my husband pulled into the emergency department, my oldest son, Vincent, who Charles had left with, came running toward me to comfort me.

I was a mess, and Vincent said to me, "Mama, stop crying. Chucky is fine."

I asked, "Are you sure?"

He responded, "Yes, ma'am."

Minutes later, my sister Carol arrived trembling, yet trying to hold it together for me. While we were waiting on the doctor to come out and talk to us, I know I walked the emergency door entrance at least a hundred times, pacing back and forth. My mom was at home holding everything and everybody down; meaning she was in full control of the situation while she waited for my brother, who is also my pastor, to come relieve her so that she could come and be with her grandson and me. My husband came out to where I was and said, "The doctor would like for us to come to the conference room."

My dad, son, sister, and I walked with my husband to the room where the doctor was being accompanied by several others. Seeing all of these people, I immediately felt an urgency to empty my bladder. I told the doctor that I was going to use the restroom, which was right inside of the conference room, and that I give him permission to update my family on Charles's condition. As I began washing my hands, I heard a lot of screaming, yelling, and hollering.

When I opened the door I saw Vincent lying on the floor with policemen surrounding him. I looked at my sister and asked, "Chucky's gone?"

She frantically responded, "Yes."

I looked at the police and said, "I just lost one son, please don't take another one from me."

They responded, "We're trying to keep him from hurting himself."

I called my mother and said, "I need you mom. Chucky is gone."

By this time, my brother had made it to our parents' home, and my mother soon arrived at the hospital. I told my husband that I would need him, along with my dad to go back and see Chucky, and then he could tell me if I could handle seeing him. When he returned, he assured me that I could handle it. He said that Chucky looked as if he was sleeping. My mother and I walked hand in hand back to where Chucky was.

When I saw him, I began crying while kissing all over his face, asking him over and over again, "Why did you leave me?"

My mother held me in her arms and said, "Baby, after seeing what he has seen and as much as he loves you, he wouldn't come back here for anything in the world."

Immediately I felt calm and confused simultaneously. When I came from the back, my supervisor, who was then and still remains genuinely dear to me, was sitting in the lobby, along with some of my family and friends. He said, "I want to pray for Kim and her children."

We all went out at front, formed a circle, holding hands, and he prayed for us.

Everyone was about to leave the hospital, and we were trying to decide where we would be when telling my children that Chucky died.

11

It was decided that I would deliver this horrific news to them at my parents' home where everyone was. So I got in the car with my best friend, Liz, and we were heading to my parents' home.

All of sudden, I began crying uncontrollably for my children's sake saying, "How can I tell them that their brother, who picks them up from the bus stop and who eats at the dinner table every day with us, is dead, and that we won't see him at our house again?"

I knew there was no way I could deliver that type of news to them. After all, we were once a very close family, and people were always admiring our relationship.

When we pulled up at my parents' home, I got out of the car, went in, and told my mom that I wouldn't be able to break this kind of news to my children and that I would need for her to do it. I walked out and closed the door behind me. As I sat in the car, maybe all of what seemed to be five minutes had gone by when I began hearing screaming from my babies and seeing other family members running out the house hysterically. I got out of the car and went back into my parents' home to console my children. Now it was around 7:00 p.m., and we were headed across the street to my house. It was filled from the front yard and throughout the house with so many people who loved Chucky and whose lives he had touched in such remarkable ways.

Before I would reach the front yard, my brother/pastor caught up to me. He held me in his arms, I smiled at him and told him just how good God is.

He looked at me and said, "Kim, you remind me of Job, your faith is strong even in this."

Then he went on to say how Job had lost everything and still remained faithful. After such a long night of hugs, kisses, tears, conversations, and dining, my husband, children, and I went to bed. Before going to bed, I got down on my knees and asked God to forgive those young guys who killed my Chucky and for strength that I may forgive them also.

Somewhere in the night, Satan tried to subdue me. I was actually fighting him with all of my strength, but I was beginning to grow tired. All at once, I remembered that I couldn't fight him off in my own strength and that at the name of Jesus, demons flee. As I inwardly called the name of Jesus, the grip that Satan had on me began to dwindle. It was like in the movie *The Wizard of Oz* when they threw water on the wicked witch, and she began to melt.

Well this was my experience, the only difference is that this was very real. When I came through and had fully awakened, my husband in a loud, concerned voice asked me if I was okay. As I began to tell him what I had just gone through, he told me I was kicking as if I was in a fight. We both prayed together and asked God for a peaceful sleep, and I slept like a baby.

Charles died five days before my thirty-seventh birthday and seven days before my wedding anniversary. The next morning, I was up early as usual. This was normal for me since I worked first shift. After getting myself prepared for the day, I went downstairs, sat in the kitchen, and watched the news.

In the middle of watching the news, my telephone rang, it was my close friend Madelyn. She expressed to me how sad she was when she saw the news report. We began to laugh about how, when Chucky was about three years old, she came back into our lives and fell in love with him all over again.

She said, "I'll never forget the day when we were in your bedroom. I took his ball and told him it was mine. He looked at me with those pretty glossy eyes and that head full of curly hair and said, 'Give me my ball.' Then he looked at you and said, 'Mama get it.'"

So many memories from everyone, too many to count, as everyone would repeat those same words, "Charles loved his mama," and how inseparable we were.

As the day went by, my house was filled with so many people that I couldn't count. I remember telling them how one day, while we were all in the kitchen, I heard Charles singing a gospel song and how shocked I was. Although Chucky was raised in church, he wasn't as involved in activities as my other children because he was more on the quiet, shy side. However, at home we were used to hearing those booty popping songs ringing out from Chucky's bedroom. For the life of me, I couldn't think of what that gospel song was that I heard him singing, and my mom said for me not to worry about it that it'll

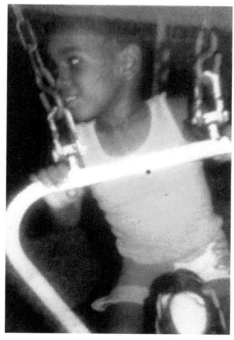

come to me. Sure thing, wouldn't you know, I was at the beauty shop that next day sitting in the chair conversing with my beautician and other clients while 104.9 played in the background. The song "You're The Reason Why I Sing" by Kirk Franklin began playing.

With joy running through me and a big smile on my face, I yelled out, "That's it! That's the song my baby was singing!" I was told by his school family that Charles used to walk the halls singing that song daily. That song would later be sung at his funeral by his friend's family.

I was taught to, "Train up a child in the way he should go and when he is old, he will not depart from it." I am grateful to know for myself that Charles had a personal relationship with God. Although he jammed to what folk trying to look like church would call secular music, you know worldly music, what we had been told for many years would send us to hell. Well, I'll have you to know that Charles was saved.

The next morning, we got dressed for Sunday morning service. It was either before or after my brother preached that he called for my husband, our children, and me to come down to the altar for a prayer. As we came down, he asked that the entire congregation would come and gather around us as he prayed. Fervent prayer will keep you together, but that's only if you want to be kept.

Monday morning, we went to Granberry Mortuary and made the arrangements. That made me numb. Later that evening, my mom, along with my siblings sat around my dining room table and prepared the obituary. That was extremely difficult for me to sit through. Although I wanted all of his accolades mentioned in the obituary, and no one knew them all like I did, I just couldn't sit through that. I really wanted it not to be real. I was very much relieved once they finished. Being born into a family where our father was a music professor, song writer, and recording artist, we're all singers. Someone in the room began singing one of those old gospels that you feel deep down within, and I started crying as if for the first time at that moment I realized that Charles was never coming back to our home and that this was real. One of my sisters Andrea or Carol helped me upstairs, put me to bed, and I so easily slept until the next morning which was my birthday.

My friend Liz surprised me with barbecue and a large spread that she had prepared. A few hours later, a couple of my sisters, some friends, coworkers, and I went to one of the neighborhood bars where I would sometimes go. When my mom got a word that I was at a bar, she was livid and sent my sister Sandra to come get me out of that bar. She told Sandra that I have no business at a place like that in a time like this. Therefore, we all left the bar and went home, but not before stopping at the liquor store where I purchased a fifth of cognac. I was drinking from one of those cups with a lid on it that never got empty. It was another late night, we were up longer than we had anticipated, but once everyone left, we went to bed.

The following morning, which is referred to as "Hump Day Wednesday" was busy nonstop. My children were running in and out, going to the malls having shirts made, and making sure that they were prepared for Charles's visitation which would take place on Thursday, May 20—my husband and my anniversary. Our home was like Grand Central Station, people were bringing in food, cards, flowers, you name it, and everyone played a roll.

Around twelve-thirty that afternoon, my husband and I went to the funeral home to drop off Charles's clothes. As I write this line, I debate with myself rather or not it was me who took his clothes inside. Although I wasn't sure, the more I wrote with tears rolling down my face, I was convinced that I did not take his clothes in—it was my husband. I loved taking care of Chucky.

He wore the finest gear from head to foot and his favorite line was, "I stay fresh."

This wasn't as if I was about to have him try on one of those Easter suits when he was a young man, or me waiting to see him in one of his fresh fits after getting ready for his school's homecoming. This was his funeral. Underclothes, socks, suit; everything that he was to be wearing in his casket, so there's no way I took his clothes in. I sat out in the car while my husband took his things in. As we drove back to the house, I began feeling very sad, but nobody knew it because I wore a smile on my face.

THE STORY THAT MUST BE TOLD

THE STORY THAT MUST BE TOLD

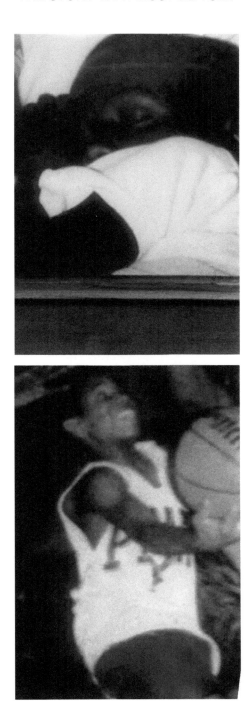

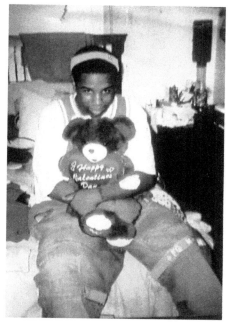

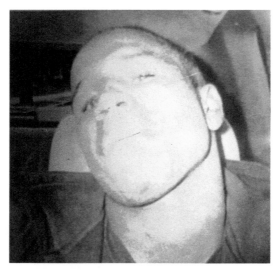

Here we are, Thursday, the twentieth of May, a whole week since I've seen my baby and the day now begins. Vincent had to be at the funeral home that morning so that he could cut Chucky's hair. He was Chucky's primary barber. My sister Sandra accompanied Vincent in the room where he cut his brother's hair. I was more concern about how Vincent would hold up after seeing his brother for the first time since his passing. After all, Chucky was his little brother even though they were only one year apart. My two daughters and I had an appointment with my beautician that morning. We were to be at the funeral home at 2:00 p.m. (two hours before the visitation started), which was from 4:00 p.m. to 8:00 p.m. I was to make sure that Charles was well put together before anyone else arrived.

Once I was there, no one could pry me from his side. Before my children and I left home to go to the funeral home, I had a very intense conversation with them about how we were not going to cry or show any lack of faith. I told them to remember that God allowed Chucky to leave here and that we would not mourn as those who do not know Christ. Because we know that to be absent from the body is to be present with the Lord. We wouldn't behave as those who don't have hope.

My children had always trusted my faith and how I operated as their mother. But today, after all that has transpired, and with many conversations years later with my children about how I instructed them to behave, I regret not allowing them to express how they really felt.

Charles's funeral was held at our church the next day at 10:00 a.m. I was up and dressed sitting on my porch as early as 9:00 a.m. waiting for everyone to arrive. We were loved by so many people, and we had family members coming from all over—New York, Michigan, Chicago, Atlanta, Arizona, and Wisconsin, just to name a few. There were many wonderful words spoken about Charles, a lot of crying, and I felt so bad for their hurt.

My brother did the eulogy. He preached from the fifth chapter of St. Mark about the man whose name was Legion. By the end of this book, you would come to see how I too entered there. My children were obedient to my instructions when they viewed their brother for the last time, but my husband was torn up from the floor up, and I felt so sorry for him. I was the last one to view Charles with my mom and dad by my side.

Chucky, so handsome, I smiled at him, kissed those lips, and all over his face before my dad, who worked at the funeral home, would close the casket for the last time. There were more than six hundred people at his funeral, and over half followed us to Lake Charles Cemetery, including school buses. It was in the car ride to his final destination that I broke down. I couldn't believe what was happening, or what had happened. No one other than my children and the chauffer knew that I had broken down, and before I got out the car, I apologized over and over again for my breakdown.

When we arrived and exited the car, I was once again wearing that smile. Once we were seated and everyone else was in place, I suddenly began singing these lyrics, "I am so grateful / That I have Christ, He's in my life. What would my life be without Him? / It would be very dark and drear. / For when I'm sad He cheers me, / And when I'm lonely He will my comfort be / That's why I'm grateful truly grateful I'm so grateful that I have Christ He's in my life." I sung those lyrics twice.

I didn't want it to end, but I knew that we couldn't stay there all day. After we left the repast, people began to fill my house again. After having to leave my baby at the cemetery, I was mentally and physically drained. I came in, got in bed, and there I stayed until the following afternoon.

As days went by, I would focus on Chucky's voice. I tried so hard not to forget how he'd stretch "Ma-Ma" when he would call me, and I tried to hold on to his scent.

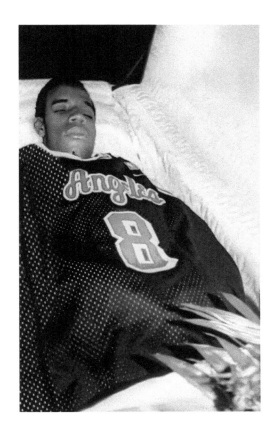

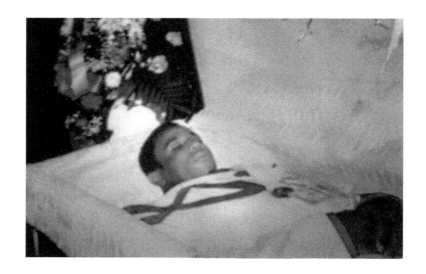

CHAPTER 2

Lost and Turned Out

Being on work-leave for more than a year afforded me bad decisions which would be attached to awful consequences that would last for what seemed like a lifetime. There was a bar that sat directly in the back of my house. I would go there some days for hours at a time, drinking and throwing darts mostly by myself.

On the 12th of June, less than a month after Chucky's death, I met a man there. He sent me a drink by the bar attendant. I accepted, but I sent him a message through her that was, "I am not in a social mood. I buried my son less than a month ago, but I do appreciate the drink."

I know I might've been in the bar at least five hours when Liz walked in. She, being my best friend for no less than twenty-five years, could sense that I was in my own zone, so she came and sat at the table and just watched me throw darts for a while. After a while, she asked me if she could join me, and it was fine for we use to throw darts against one another and against our children. Watching me from across the room and seeing how I was laughing while bonding with my friend, the guy from earlier, who had sent the drink, thought it was the appropriate time to come over and introduce himself to me.

He expressed how sorry he was for my loss and soon after, he would leave the bar but not before leaving his telephone number and money for more drinks. It was two weeks until he would hear from me, and it came after another argument that my husband and I had, concerning his over-impulsiveness. It wasn't much longer that this man and I entered into a relationship, and I was asking my husband for a divorce after thirteen years. I thought that I had seen it all. I'm thirty-seven, had been married twice, shot by my first husband at the early age of seventeen, and had buried one of my six children. "Shiggady," I thought my life was over, and I had better take my chances with this man who was thirty years older than me and had proclaimed to love me, and wanted to make me his wife.

Lord, have mercy; that was a lot.

Within a year of us being together, he sold his county home and bought us a $300,000 house in the city. I was so elated for all of one month. It didn't take long for the newness of this house to wear off, and soon I had begun feeling like I had excluded Chucky by leaving the house where every joy and memory I had of him resided. I felt as if I had turned my back on my son. My guy and I began arguing daily because I had become depressed talking about how upset I was that Chucky was no longer on this earth.

He began saying things to me like, "I thought you were okay. You have always said that God loves your son and that he's at peace."

Every day, I would hear this man remind me of what I had said to him and this would make me so mad. So one day, I told God, "Look, I know that You love me, and You know that I love You, but I will not pray to You or have any more conversations with You because I want to grieve my baby. I know that if I continue my intimacy with You, then You would keep me, and I don't want to be kept."

I really did mean exactly what I had said. *Big, huge, pricey mistake*! Everything that Satan had, he came at me with it.

In this new house were two bars: one in the basement where I threw darts for hours, and the other in the kitchen where I prepared daily meals. In the house were gallons of alcohol, "shiggady," you name it, we had it. I was drinking from sun up until sun down even when I was working.

My old man had begun noticing bottles diminishing from the bar at a rapid pace. One day, he sat me down and said, "Anything I put in the house is for you, but I am very concern about the amount of alcohol that you have been consuming. It appears as if you' re consuming at least a couple of gallons a week."

I was embarrassed, ashamed, and defensive all at the same time. See, what I would do when a bottle became empty was have one of my children take it out of the house and put it in a dumpster away from the house, just in case my old man would happen to be throwing something out and stumble upon a familiar product. I had become verbally abusive toward him while still trying to keep up this charade like I was holding it together. I was putting up this image in front of my family and friends like we were happy after we had been in our house for three months.

However, things were terrible between us due to my behavior, regardless of every attempt by him to make me happy. Saturday, October 1, 2005, after leaving work, I called Liz and told her that I wanted to go to a bar and that I was on a mission to meet someone new.

First she said, "No, Kim, that's not who you are."

However, once I convinced her that I wouldn't jeopardize my integrity and that I only wanted to throw darts, she agreed to come with me. Two weeks prior, my baby girl, Jabria and I flew to Minnesota for her sixteenth birthday. We were there for four days and three nights. Although I had planned this trip months in advance, looking for my baby girl to shop until she was satisfied (because money wasn't an issue). I also told Liz and my boss that I was seeking a new relationship and was hoping that it would happen while in Minnesota.

They both pleaded with me saying, "Kim, I know that things have been bleak at home, but I won't sit back and watch you lose all of your dignity and destroy who you are in the midst. You don't need a man to fill the void of Chucky, and if you feel that bad then go back to your house where you can begin to heal."

Tears began rolling down my face as I would listen to both of them at different times. I took their advice of not getting involved with anyone, but I didn't move back home.

On the Saturday after work that she agreed to go to the bar with me, I met a guy. He was not my type at first sight and not someone I would've entertained on a good day or in good times. He kept talking to me, but when he told me where he worked and that he was one of my closest friend's supervisor, I thought this to be fate. Where he worked, he wore a uniform and as crazy as this may sound, I thought that he was the one, being that my Chucky wore a military uniform every day at his school.

Yes, I do admit that I was very delusional, and my condition wasn't apparent to my loved ones, and those that I was around daily. For three years, I put on this front as if I was still the life of the party. See, before Chucky died, I would throw big parties, supplying everything that one would need, was involved in many activities, and freely gave my time and finances in church and family events. Your all-around sweet, loving person, and no one knew that I was dying from the inside out. There were many times while driving I had to pull over because I couldn't see the road due to my tears. While other times, Satan would tell me to just drive off the road and end it all.

A coworker and I became very close on the evening that Charles died. I saw her daily at work in passing, and we would only speak to one another, but when Charles died, she showed great compassion. She was at my house every day, and when the funeral service was over, she would call me every day. I began calling her during the day while she was working, she never said that she couldn't listen to me. I would cry and so would she.

Her mother, children, and extended family welcomed me as if I was one of their own. I had begun a relationship with the man in the uniform while still living in the house with the older man. I knew that someday, I would return back to my home ending the relationship with the older man, but I just didn't know when, only because my children were really enjoying what was supposed to be their new home.

I would go and check on my house at least once a week, not concerned that someone would even entertain the thought of breaking into my house, let alone committing the act. We had lived on this block since 1979 and had never had a break-in. We bought three more homes on this same block, but January 6, 2006, when I did my random check, I noticed my back door ajar. My heart immediately began racing because I knew in that instance that my house had been violated. I didn't go in until the police arrived.

Several of my large expensive items had been stolen but were later returned that same day from my neighbor's basement. Chucky's bedroom had been dismantled and all of his belongings that I kept were gone—including his play station that he enjoyed playing daily, television, games, expensive one-of-a-kind jerseys, several pairs of his basketball shoes, and caps.

I was furious! Knowing that somewhere out there, someone had my son's things that he worked so hard to achieve caused me to have a breakdown. My children seeing me in this state caused them to go into a rage which made them adamant about finding Chucky's things.

My sister Lynette, being concern about what she was hearing coming from my children's mouths, shouted out without thinking, "They're just things!"

I became very abusive with my language and was shouting out things like, "You pretended to love my son and all these years have been an act!"

I was making accusations that people were jealous of me and my children's relationship for years. Hurt, ashamed, and confused, all these emotions taking presence caused me to be bitter and withdrawn from those who had been around me since the beginning.

From that moment on, I was really confused and had started blaming myself saying, "If I would have never left my home then this would not have happened, and Chucky's things would still be here."

I was emotionally distraught and now had the headache of repairing my house. So much was happening all at once. I would contemplate week after week about moving back home because somewhere deep within, I knew what I was doing was wrong, but the more I mourned, the more I would drink, and the more I drank, the more careless I became.

There were several incidents that came into play, but the one when I knew that it was time for me to leave was Super Bowl Sunday 2006. My guy and I had plans to go to a Super Bowl party, but that afternoon, I told him that I had changed my mind and that I was going to stay in and watch the game with my children.

We exchanged words, and as the day progressed, he left for the party. I was thinking that I was being careful by waiting until half time before leaving the house to go and meet my new friend at the bar. So when the game was over, he and I left the bar, and I followed him to his place not knowing that I was also being followed.

My friend lived in a twelve-story apartment complex, and my guy didn't know exactly which apartment I had entered. When he called my phone and told me where I was, I became alarmed. I was afraid for my life not knowing if he would harm me. My children were there at the house, and I believed that he wouldn't do anything to hurt them, and though I wasn't 100 percent sure, I stayed the night at my friend's house until the next day. When I arrived at the house, my guy and I had an extensive conversation about my behavior, and I admitted to nothing. Of course, once again, I lied. I was scheduled to have surgery on March 6, 2006.

I knew that I wanted to be back in my house by then. I would repeat to my friend at least once a week how I wasn't moving back home so that we could be together. I was getting away from where I didn't want to be. The clock was ticking. Only four weeks until my surgery, I began moving small items out of the house so that he wouldn't notice and ask me to leave before I was actually ready to leave.

CHAPTER 3

Too Much Pain

I was finally home within a couple of days after my surgery. I was so happy, but I had work to do because of the break-in. Within a couple of weeks, I had most of my things repaired, but there was still a great void, and I cried every day. I blamed myself for letting Chucky leave the day that he was killed because I had first told him that he could not go, but he's being persistent. I said as I still remember those words today, "Okay Chucky, you can go."

He smiled at me, and they pulled off. That scene tormented me for many years. I was in so much pain that I had become verbally and physically abusive to both my new friend and my children. No one knew, was just too cowardly to speak up, or just had been looking like church all this time, lacking discernment of what was taking place—Satan had taken over.

I remember telling my oldest daughter, Katrina that my baby girl, Jabria was walking around the house on this particular Saturday morning as if she had an attitude knowing that, that behavior is unacceptable. Never do Kim's kids portray such a disrespectful, distasteful image. Katrina, being that bold outspoken daughter she's always been, took a deep breath and said, "Mama, I wouldn't have anything to say to you either had you done to me what you did to her."

When I asked what I had done, she looked at me as if she was stunned and said, "Mama you don't remember?"

I replied, "Remember what?"

Katrina said, "Not only did you verbally abuse my sister, but you choked my sister, and now she can barely talk." I was feeling really bad about what I had done, but the more Katrina talked about some kind of intervention for me, the angrier and more defensive I became. I began believing my justifications for why I did what I did.

A few months earlier, my good paying automotive job, where I had been employed for seven years, left St. Louis and went overseas. This was a great loss for me. I was trying to maintain like I had always done—not missing a beat, and eventually, I went down and everyone was able to see it. November of that same year, I felt as if I had had enough torment. It was two weeks before Thanksgiving, Wednesday night prayer. I decided that nothing was going to stop me from going to prayer at my place of worship where I had been absent.

I got there early about forty-five minutes before the actual start time. My uncle, who is also a deacon, was eating in the fellowship hall. When I walked in, he's being happy to see me, invited me to the table where he was. With tears rolling down my face and snot running from my nose, he would be the first one I would tell how I had walked away from God.

September 2005 and now for a little over two years, I felt like I was in hell. He asked the one question that many have asked me since then and even now, "Kim, so were you angry with God?"

Some have said, "I get it. You were angry with God for taking your son."

My response then and now still remains, "I've never been angry at God. I can't even define for any of you what that feels like. He didn't take my son. The acts of Satan allowed through people, took my son. God spared not His only Son, nailed Jesus to the cross for us to be saved in this treacherous way of living. Jesus is the only Son who has laid His life down for humanity. He was then, and is still the only one worthy to do what He's done for us all. When Jesus comes back, then He will take those of us who remain, who are saved by His life that He so freely gave at the cross."

See, I've never been angry at God. God loves me, and I love Him. I just wanted to grieve for my son because in my head I thought that Chucky was saying, "Mama, how can you keep living everyday as if you're okay and keep praising and worshipping God, and I, your baby, am no longer with you?"

So I walked away from God because I began to feel like I was betraying my son by not being angry, but never was any of my anger pointed at God. This was a trick of Satan, a big mistake that I had regretted over and over again. I made the choice, and I know with everything in me that this was a costly mistake—to fall back into Satan's mess. I was persuaded that had I remained in the safety of God, that the things which took place in my children and mine lives would have never happened but because it did, God let me know years ago that I was one of His elect. He said, "I'm going to allow you to write your story just the way that it happened, and my people will see that if I did it for you, surely, I'm here with arms stretched out willing and waiting to do the possible for them." Hallelujah!

As I look back over the years and consider all of the bogus people, sex with various men, people I've hurt—especially my children first, family, husband, ex—and the places that I have entertained and allowed in my physical and mental space, I become overwhelmed. Still in all my mess, I, for reasons that only God knows, couldn't get away from being an advocate for how stretched out His love for us is, and that when we stay connected to Him, even in our sorrows and our self-inflicted pain, He is right there, willing and sure enough able to bring us to victory.

My sister would experience the loss of her child, and I would get to see that there was still something within me. In July 2006, a year and three months before I had cried out to God to forgive me, my sister Carol would lose her daughter to a drunk driver, hitting her head on. My sister and sister-in-law came to my house to give me that tragic news around 5:00 a.m. I was devastated and hurt for my sister. I never wanted any of my siblings to experience what I had gone through.

Once I was able to get myself together which was a few hours later, I drove to my sister's home. When I arrived, her house was full, and my sister was sitting on the sofa in her living room in a daze. She was a mess. With tears rolling down her face, I took her in my arms, told her that I love her, and then I said these words, "Whatever you do, don't walk away from God."

With tears rolling down her face, she said to me, "Kim, I promise you, I won't." I can honestly say that my sister have not walked away from her promise, no matter how challenging, lonesome, and many tears she's had to wipe away while raising her daughter's three children.

I believe that day was a starting point and a reminder to me of God's power. From that night in November 2007, after much sincere repentance and emptying out to God, I began feeling a release on my life. It didn't happen all at once, but I began feeling a good positive change in my mind and heart.

February 13, 2008, on my eldest son's birthday, my father passed away at my parent's home across the street from me. Now you talk about mad, "shiggady," I was mad at my daddy for leaving me, and I screamed so loud around 2:00 a.m. on their front. My dad was known as a "gentle giant" not only to my mother and his children, but to everyone that he encountered. My dad and I could talk about anything.

While people would like to say that I was spoiled, I beg to differ. I just refer to myself as "daddy's girl" which we all were in our own right. My daddy was proud of his children and grandchildren. Whenever my dad would converse with someone new or old, this is what you were guaranteed to hear: how many children he had, where we all worked, how proud he was of his grandchildren, and his wonderful, respectful relationships he had with his children's spouses.

How I so love my dad! Although I was sad when my father passed away, I rejoiced in knowing that my father was now present with the God he and my mother have taught me about. All at once, I was at peace for Chucky and Daddy were together again. Chucky was crazy about his grandfather. I was finally able to smile again and this time it was real. Chucky's father, who was a major factor in my life, died January 3, 1987, the day that Chucky turned a month old. Chucky, never knowing his father, would somehow talk to me about his father as if he knew him.

However, I am thankful that my father was not just a grandfather but a father to my son. My father was laid to rest at the Jefferson Barracks Cemetery on February 20, 2008.

On February 25, 2008, which happens to be my sister Rita's birthday, the unimaginable happened. My son Vincent's girlfriend's three-year-old daughter died while in the care of my son. I was at the store where I had been working when I got that awful call from my grandson's, Lil Vincent's mother.

She said, "Ms. Wallace, Braziah has died, and they are questioning Vincent."

After hearing what she had said, I became discombobulated. I looked at my boss/close friend who has known my children, extended family, and me for many years. I told him what she had just told me while still holding the phone.

He said, "No, this has got to be a mistake. She's gotten it all wrong. You and your family are good people. Go and find out what's going on."

Immediately, I left and went home. I isolated myself until I could deal with the big picture. As I pulled into my driveway and exited my car, I noticed several vehicles parked out in front of my parents' home that were my siblings', along with adult nieces and nephews. I was sad and mad simultaneously that an incident involving my child had taken place at a time when we were to be reflecting upon the good times with our dad.

I called my mom to find out what was going on because she and Vincent have a special bond and although she only knew the same as I had been told, she assured me that we were going to get to the bottom of this preposterous story. She told me that my brother/pastor and her brother were at the hospital where the baby had been pronounced dead.

There was so much wickedness running through my head that I said to God, "Look, I know that You did not allow me to have four sons and to bring them up pursuing Your will for their lives for this kind of stuff to keep happening."

Then I heard very calmly, "Train up a child in the way he should go: and when he is old, he will not depart."

I immediately knew that this was another one of Satan's tricks to get into my mind in order to get me to walk away from God a second time. I knew then, that regardless to what Satan was trying to get me to believe, my son belonged to God and that he wouldn't hurt a child for anything in this world. Satan and I were literally arguing because he was trying to convince me that I should be denouncing God.

Satan was saying to me, "You have a son dead, and now a son that's a murderer, and you still believe in this God?"

I told that evil, conniving, jealous bastard that the only way that any person could think that my son could do an unthinkable act would be because he, as cunning as he is, has convinced them of it by gaining full control of their minds.

The detectives had taken Vincent back to the house to do a reenactment and afterward he was free to go. I didn't, and I knew that I couldn't stop praising God. I knew that God would be glorified in it all. Satan has had it out for me, trying to destroy me since before I was five years of age. Although I keep getting off course every time something new comes along, I remain determined to see the work that God has begun in me to its completion.

Vincent and his girlfriend stayed a few nights with her family and my family because they were unable to bring themselves back to the place where Braziah had died.

A few days later, Vincent had to be hospitalized for the third time due to him sustaining two gunshot wounds to the back, one month before Braziah's death. Someone had attempted to rob Vincent because of the drug trafficking lifestyle he lived and during this attempt, he was shot. I was not a mother who condoned this kind of behavior, and when Vincent would come over to the house, we had good family time.

July 4, 2008, I held a special gala for my family and neighbors. Everyone had a fantastic time: enjoying pony rides, bounce house, face painting, music, and plenty of food. Toward the end of the night we had a balloon release in honor of those who had died which also included Braziah released by her mother.

July 29, 2008, Vincent and his girlfriend visited with us for Sunday morning service, and after service they came over for dinner. I had cooked greens, homemade macaroni and cheese, potato salad, some kind of meat (what kind exactly I'm not sure), etc. Yes, I am known for my delicious meals but not just on Sundays; however, this was good for we enjoyed bonding all day. It would be less than twenty-four hours standing in the kitchen where we had enjoyed Sunday dinner that I would get this horrifying call from my son Vincent, telling me that he's at the police headquarters being interrogated by detectives about Braziah's death.

I was freaking livid! My response was, "What the hell?"

Then I said to him, "Let me call Grandmama" (my mother).

She told us that she would call my brother, which she did, and that same evening my son was charged with first degree murder with a $500,000 cash only bond attached to it. Vincent knew that he was hated by a few within the justice system due to his drug trafficking. He had even been told by at least one officer that they would eventually get something that would stick, but murder, he or any of us never saw this one coming.

I couldn't believe that this was happening. My hands were tied, and I didn't know what to do. I wanted to use my house as collateral but found out that I couldn't due to the terms of the bond. I had stopped watching the news due to how the media was parading Vincent's picture across the screen as a baby killer. Seeing Vincent on the news and in the papers caused me to become weak. My phone would ring nonstop, and although I knew that these allegations were false, I was ashamed, angry, and sick to my stomach, but the one thing that I didn't do was walk away from God. I didn't want to leave my house because you see, my children and I are well known, and so I wanted to stay away from the public.

While I was trying to protect my children from anyone's questions or remarks, my baby girl, Jabria was trying to keep me from seeing what was on the front of the newspapers in our neighborhood stores. I'll never forget the one day that I did leave the house accompanied by my two youngest sons going to the store to purchase a pack of cigarettes. The owner happened to be an upstanding guy, and he was also my friend, so I knew that we were on safe ground. As we exited the car, I was approached by a very close male friend of mine, Red who has since died. I had my sons to go into the store while I talked to Red. When we finished talking, I went into the store, paid for my cigarettes, and my sons and I left out together. When I pulled off and turned the corner, my son, Andre said, "Mama, Mr. Fred was asking us about Vincent being in jail, and he said that if we need anything we could ask him."

I immediately made a U-turn and went back to the store, but this time the three of us walked in together. My blood was boiling, and I could hear my heart beating. I was later told by my friend, Red who was still in the store waiting to run errands for Fred, the store owner, that my eyes were bloodshot red. I walked up to Fred and told him that he had better not ever approach my children about anything and that they don't need a damn thing from him. I said a few more things, and then we walked out.

CHAPTER 4

Could This Be Our There

After some days had gone by, my son and I agreed that I'd come see him. I knew nothing about visiting someone in jail, and although my sister Sandra and my boyfriend, Jeff worked there, I was still miserable. Seeing my son for the first time, behind that thick glass, I thought I would die. He and I cried during this visit because neither one of us could make sense as to what was happening. Some of the correctional officers would treat me as if I was a criminal, and this would cause me to defend my character which resulted in me being denied a visit with my son a couple of times. See, I didn't request special privilege for my son or me, so no one knew who we were related to until it was almost time for his trial. However, my son, the correctional officers, and my relationship had flourished beautifully which caused us to have a great deal of respect for one another. For two years, my weekends were interrupted due to visits with my son, but always when my boyfriend was off from work in order to keep from bringing anymore unnecessary embarrassment to myself.

There were times that my boyfriend and I would see each other in the lobby when he had to stay over until his relief arrived. He would avoid making eye contact or conversing with me like I had seen him do with others who he knew that were coming to see their loved ones. He would act as if he was ashamed for anyone to know that he knew us and that he lived in my home at least four nights a week. For seven years (2006–2013), he was with me at every family reunion, funeral, and other family functions in and out of town, but I allowed myself to be mistreated not realizing my worth because of what I thought my condition was.

There were times that I took Vincent's children to visit him and these were sad visits. Vincent was very active in his children's lives. On Monday, the day Braziah died, Vincent Jr. was there and had been with his dad the entire weekend, and his mother was to pick him up for school that afternoon. His daughter, Vintasia, had also been over at the house with her dad, but she had gone home that Friday. When Vincent Jr. would say to his dad that he was going to break that glass and get him from back there, I would get choked up and feel hurt for my son and grandchildren.

My son and I had many visits with just the two of us and because of his strong faith in God, my heart would always be made glad. Regardless of the drug trafficking choice that Vincent may have made, he was taught about God and knew Him for himself. I looked forward to these visits because Vincent and I would sing, pray, and he would give me a good Bible lesson all within those forty-five minutes. There were many times when all of my children, along with Vincent were still living at home that we would have Bible study in our home, and Vincent would take over our Bible study for he knew more about the Bible than I had ever claimed.

Though I've had many ups and downs in the earlier years in life, my faith in God had always caused me to triumph. Earlier, I mentioned that I had been shot. I was seventeen years young with a baby. Thinking that I knew more than my parents, I married a guy against my parents' wishes, who was at least eight years older than me. Six months later, while being pregnant with Vincent, my husband shot me from behind with a sawed-off shotgun. I was sitting on the bed and was seven months pregnant. The bullet hit me in my left arm, right above my elbow, with no less than fifty exploding pellets from the bullet, splattering into my lower right arm and the wall without one pellet ever touching my stomach. Vincent was protected because of God's favor on my and Vincent's life. Although I had never become disrespectful to my parents, or my elders, I was rebellious—a very fast young girl and lady.

This was caused by the appetite for sex, due to being violated by someone outside of my immediate family when I was just a fragile—four-year-old child. I never stopped talking to God through it all. There were many times throughout my young marriage when I was used as bullet target practice, but God was the shield around me. Satan has tried to kill, steal, and destroy me, but God has made me promises for right here and right now on earth that extends to my children, their children, and so on. For these reasons, I will not throw in the towel.

The weeks leading up to Vincent's trial, I was so happy for I knew that he was innocent and that, that Thanksgiving would be the last holiday spent without his presence at the table. We were 100 percent sure that we would be celebrating Christmas together as we had always done in the past. Vincent had gained so much weight, so I asked my uncle if he could loan him one of his suits to wear during trial. Without any hesitation, my uncle willingly gave up his suit while my brother offered him a white shirt and tie. This was not to impress or throw anyone off for this was the appropriate attire that I would have him wear. I must admit that Vincent looked darn good to me. It had been almost two years that I'd finally seen him from behind that glass, and this time, out of that prison jumpsuit and into something more acceptable. I was finally allowed to touch my son.

It was December 19, 2010, the first day of his trial. My family, friends, church members, and I sat for hours, listening to opening arguments, not really sure as to what was going on. This was my first encounter with something of this magnitude where my child was being accused of murder, let alone in any courtroom case involving him at all. I couldn't afford an attorney on my own, so he was appointed a public defender. I didn't know that public defenders are owned by the state, not that it would have made any difference as to my ability to pay for an attorney, or my understanding of the juridical system. The juridical system offers public defenders, not as a means of fairness, but allows our so called justice system full control of what is and is not admissible during trial.

However, had I known that back then, I still would have trusted that these people that I voted into office would be true. There were vital, undeniable evidence withheld from the jurors which included, but not limited to the fact that Vincent called and talked with a 911 operator, and she instructed him on how to give cardiopulmonary resuscitation (CPR). You could hear him performing this action. There was also a video of the same day reenactment tape, but this was also information that our justice system didn't make known to the jurors. Braziah had been taken to the hospital the year prior, February 2007 for the disease gastroenteritis which causes inflammation to the stomach and intestines, typically resulting from bacteria toxins of viral infection and causing vomiting and diarrhea. According to *Encyclopedia of Children's Health*, "Viral gastroenteritis is one of the most common, acute (sudden-onset) illnesses in the United States with millions of cases reported annually. Each year, an estimated two hundred thousand children younger than age five are hospitalized with gastroenteritis symptoms. Of these children, three hundred die as a result of severe diarrhea and dehydration. In developing nations, diarrheal illnesses are a major source of mortality." This is the information that I've been made aware of since the trial, and now know how important it was. I knew that my son was innocent and had done nothing but tried to help this baby live.

It was Friday, the fifth day of trial, which would be the last day for this case as instructed by the judge earlier in the week. We heard closing arguments from both the defense and prosecution team. I smiled at Vincent and gave him a kiss after the jurors went out of the court room to discuss their verdict. I knew in my heart that Vincent, now at age twenty-four, was coming home that day. It was around

4:00 p.m., and we were told that the jurors had reached their verdict. *Nervous, serious* and *focused* were we, as we, his family walked back into the courtroom hand in hand. We sat down in total quietness.

The jurors read, "We the jurors find . . . guilty of murder in the second degree and child abuse resulting in death." I ran out the courtroom into the corridor and into a phone booth daring anyone to come near me. You know the story of Adam and Eve, and how they both hid (condemned themselves) because (sin) they disobeyed God, and they realized that they were naked? Well, I knew that Vincent had done absolutely no wrong, but I felt so ashamed (condemned) because I felt that I (self-gratification) had done everything right, for the most part, in raising my children. Vincent told his younger brother Andre, "Go and be with Mother."

This is what I was later told. As we all convened in the lobby in such disbelief, we were asking his defense, "What now, how do we help Vincent?"

The officers were he had been housed for two years, believed in his innocence, and they were sad with me. One of the nurses there at the jail, who was also a pastor that had the pleasure of conversing with Vincent on a regular basis, was overcome with grief on the day of the verdict. He had to evaluate Vincent while he was placed on suicide watch which is standard procedure for everyone found guilty on a high profile case.

During the evaluation process, the nurse was so overcome with pity that he could barely speak. Vincent said to him, "Where is your faith? Don't you trust God? I know that you're not going to give up now."

Those were the same words I heard when he called me that evening. For everyone who was crying, Vincent's powerful prayer brought peace to our hearts, and we were able to regroup. The following Friday was Christmas. We waited until the first part of the year to discuss with his defense team as to what he was up against in terms of years, or if anything at all, according to my faith.

February 19, 2010, was the day of Vincent's sentencing, which also happened to be the exact date but three years prior, that Braziah was diagnosed with the disease gastroenteritis. Before we walked into the court room, we all held hands and prayed. I remember my mother speaking on Vincent's behalf and the judge reading the letter that I had submitted but what the judge would say next almost sent me to a psychiatric hospital.

The judge uttered, "Twenty-five years in a maximum prison."

While trying to hold it together for Vincent and my other children, my whole body became numb. I became angry at everyone, more so my man who worked at the jail and was not as supportive as I would have liked him to be during the two years of this difficult time. I was so quiet that no one was able to depict the anger that was inside of me. As I left the courtroom, I felt that life with my son as I've always known it to be was over.

I walked in my house and took an eight by ten framed picture of Vincent off the piano and took it to my bedroom. I got in my bed, curled up in a fetal position with Vincent's picture pressed to my heart, as if it was him, and wouldn't let go. Then my sister Carol, whom Charles had named Ms. Drama Queen, came into my room. Seeing me that way, she began to sob. Quickly, my other sister Sandra came in, pulled me out of bed, and began praying. We left my room, she stretched my arms up and out, and she began to sing, "Father I stretch my hands to Thee, / no other help I know / If Thou withdraw Thyself from me, / oh, whither shall I go?"

I tell you, it's something about those old spiritual songs that reaches your soul. When you have a relationship with God, can't a devil in hell keep you from receiving that which God has for you. I began singing those lyrics while reflecting back in my mind how God had rescued me out of the miry clay a couple of years earlier, after I had cried out to Him. As I continued singing, those tears changed from tears of sadness to tears of calmness. I am forever thankful to my sister for not allowing me to become trapped in Satan's web. By this time, I had built up an appetite, so I went downstairs where everybody was and dined.

Over the next few months, Vincent remained downtown at the jail waiting to be moved to where he would spend his time. I worked tirelessly selling dinners and other perishable items, hoping to raise enough money to attain a lawyer for Vincent's appeal. There was an organization that started "The Coalition to Free Vincent." The more money I made, the more money I spent on interviews with news reporters, hoping that someone would read the newspapers and help me help my son after reading his story. I went to a lot of meetings and supported people financially in similar cases. To top it off, it seemed like every Friday, which was usually my going to the bar night, Vincent would call me to tell me about a prophet who was going to be at a hotel, or at a church and that he needed his siblings and me to be there and to be on time. He always told me that I was to be one of those who gave a special offering, and each time yes, I was until I had depleted all I had saved.

CHAPTER 5

Though I'm Missing You

Early spring, April 20, 2011, Vincent was moved to Bonne Terre. He called me right before he was to leave. I was so sad and crying. I told him that I love him, and he said that he loved me, and we both hung up. My man was lying next to me. He tried to console me by telling me that everything would be okay and that Vincent was going to be fine. I never allowed those words to register within. Knowing that my man had worked at the jail for many years, and my experiences with him, I felt that he felt that people learned to adapt. However, I, being Vincent's mother, knowing that he was caged like an animal with real high profile criminals made my body cringe. Not long after he was at Bonne Terre, he was moved to the South

Eastern Correctional Center in Licking, Missouri, to do the time that this unjust system has placed upon him, now making him an absent father to his children. I have come face to face, choosing Vincent's side against my other children, due to the anger he feels about being in prison for something that not only he didn't do but that never even happened. In the past, I have tried to make my children understand that when Vincent begins to vent and lash out at us for going on with our lives then, we should understand. Recently, I've come to realize that being a codependent to his pain, and we feeling guilty about trying to enjoy life does not allow him to realize that although we have not put our lives on hold, we also have not walked away from his situation as if it's over. I understood how he felt because when I was going through my hurt, which I chose to go through when I walked away from God's love, I disregarded how my actions would affect those connected to me. I felt they had moved on so easily without Charles, and for some selfish reason, I wanted people to feel guilty for going on with their lives when Charles had been denied the same.

A year after Vincent had been at Licking, the same situation that sent him to prison had now come inside my door. My great nephew, who was also my godson, had just awakened from his mid-morning nap. I was going to take him and my granddaughter to a carnival at the school I was attending. I had been watching him for several months while his mom went to work. On this particular day, my adult niece who was twenty-five years old at the time, licensed to care for children and still works in a children's center was at my home. My three-year-old nephew, my niece, and I were in the kitchen all in close proximity. I was standing at the stove while my nephew and niece sat at the kitchen table. I had cut up some hotdogs and some peaches for him to eat. I observed him only eating peaches, so I laughed, and then I said, "Let's eat the hotdogs."

After he saw me eating one of the pieces, he took one and put it in his mouth. Seconds later, I heard my niece sitting directly across from me yell, "He's choking!"

So I put my arms around him and did the Heimlich maneuver, but seeing that that wasn't working, I lifted both of his arms up while screaming for my niece to dial 911. I took my finger and put it in his mouth hoping to sweep out any particles that might be blocking his airway, when all of a sudden, I felt his teeth clamping down on my finger removing a couple layers of skin as I pulled out. With him in my arms, and me moving fast to get him out on the front porch for some air and help, I could hear Satan more than once in my ear saying, "Just throw him over on the lot. No one will know."

I knelt down to lay my god baby on my porch, but I kept him in my arms as I cried and prayed. Then all of a sudden, I saw someone coming out from my neighbor's house running across and down the street. He heard me screaming for someone to help me and ran to my rescue. Kneeling down, he took my nephew out of my arms and began CPR. I later found out that this guy, who God sent to my rescue, worked in Children's Hospital Emergency. Seeming like forever for the paramedics to arrive, my nephew/god baby was not breathing. I rode in the ambulance to the hospital with him, and my sister Lynette, who lives across the street from me, called my nephew's mother. An hour after being at the hospital, Vincent called my phone and asked me over and over again if I was all right. I could hardly talk for crying so much and apologized to him for what he had gone through all by himself with no one there to be a witness and help him. Today, my nephew is doing so well, living a full life, that if I had never told you what had happened to him, you would have never suspected. My son and I were praying while the doctors worked on him, and I know that God heard our sincere prayer.

When the doctors said that they couldn't find anything in his abdomen tracing back to what I said he had eaten, some of his mom's friends and some church attendees, turned on me as if I was lying about what had happened. All communication had ceased and this made me sad. It was at that time I felt that I was going through the exact same thing that Vincent was now in prison for.

During my nephew's stay in the hospital, I told my mother and a few others what Satan had suggested that I do with my nephew when he was literally dying in my arms. See, I keep telling you that this bastard has been trying to destroy me for a long time. I began feeling that even some of my own relatives didn't believe me and therefore,

I became angry at everyone even at my own mother. I wasn't angry with my mother for not believing me because my mother has never doubted me. I was angry with her for not being angry with my other family members for their continued relationships and conversations with those people who were spreading lies about me, and defaming my character.

The following year, my brother/pastor became ill. Vincent had always looked up to him as his spiritual father in the faith, so when this happened, it troubled me that Vincent had to endure this pain all by himself. As for my own pain, I felt lost because I would talk to my brother at least four days a week about how much I knew that God loves me, and the fact that I wanted a closer walk with God. Listening to him minister to my spirit with such powerful anointing, helped me daily as I was going through this spiritual warfare that seemed like no one understood except my brother. Over the next year, Vincent and I would have conversations about how and why we miss our three-way conversations with our beloved pastor. It wouldn't be long before Vincent would begin speaking things from other religions which would soon get me caught up to the point that I had begun second guessing the things which I had been taught and had always tried to conform to. Thanks be to God for His faithfulness which causes me to remain steadfast, unmovable, and always abounding in His word.

My son Andre loves his brother Vincent so much that they would talk on the phone, as we all did, daily, although missing the intimacy of their true brotherhood. At the tender age of sixteen, Andre moved out away from me, and my drunken ways and in with an older woman which also came with sex, money, and eventually a deceitful lifestyle. While I was having conversations with Vincent about the fast way Andre was living, Vincent was talking to Andre about how we all know that he's innocent and that he has no business being in prison, so if he's going to be out here getting money, then he needs to be getting enough to retain an attorney so that he can come home.

Andre was the minister of music at the church where he belonged. I would pray for Andre, and tum right around, and curse him out. I would tell him that God was not going to keep allowing him to play His music while he just keep on living any kind of way. Looking back on what I said, who was I to say something so untrue?

As if God, who is all *love*, would do an evil act that would cause harm to Andre in order to get his attention when in all actuality the choices we make good or bad have repercussions. Here I was, trying to scare him into living right when what I should have been doing along with praying was telling him how much God loves him and that Jesus bore all of his sins on the cross, and withholds nothing from him. Hmmm, that right there would have been enough to deter him from the life that he was living.

You know, religion had taught me in my era growing up that if you do well you get good, and if you do bad you get bad. Therefore, I was hoping that by telling him that God would punish him, he should stop his wicked behavior for he wouldn't want anything to happen causing him not to be able to play, which was what he loved doing and was very good at. Here I was, living the same way in which Andre was living, out of God's will, and God had not forsaken me. I was sexing with whomever, whenever I wanted to, drinking from sun up until sun down, letting any and everything come out of my mouth, and allowing sin to have dominion over me.

On Sunday mornings, my praises to God were real, but I must admit, I wasn't ready to give up that smokescreen life. I was always hopeful that I would get enough of God's word to carry me from Sunday to Sunday so that I wouldn't fall completely off course knowing what I would be indulging in through the week, but being afraid that I would lose Andre caused me to use this scare tactic which did not work.

One day Vincent and I were talking, and I was telling him that I believed that Andre had begun using drugs and that I was afraid of what could happen. I said, "I pray for him, and I am watching him die right before my eyes."

When I made that statement, Vincent went off. He said, "You all claim to believe in God, and you say that you pray and in that same breath you're telling me how you're watching him die. Really, Mama, that's what you see?" Then he went on to say, "Let me tell you something, I'm not out there, and God has told me that Andre is not going to die out there because He has His hands all over my little brother. Now, you choose to believe whatever you believe because of what you see."

I was mad at Vincent because of what he had said and how he said it to me, so I stopped talking to him. We went from talking at least three times a day to me not answering his calls for a couple of months. I went on telling my mother and everybody else how Vincent had encouraged Andre in his activity in order to get money for an attorney.

You know how we do. We get mad at someone for speaking the truth, so we take the situation out of context and begin gossiping and lying about the person to others that don't have anything to do with the matter at hand, and who could care less about what or who you're talking about. This is just something to make the person appear bad in the eyes of others because you're mad. This is a dangerous thing to do because not only do you poison those by feeding them your garbage, but you also taint the character of the person of whom you're referencing.

I don't condone wrong doing from anyone, especially my own children; however, I did come to understand how Andre would want to help his brother in the only way that he believed he knew how. Knowing how close my children are and how loyal I've taught and shown them to be toward each other, Andre pursuing this act didn't come as a surprise to me. Vincent wasn't only in Andre's ear, but he was also heavy on his heart. This was his big brother who had always protected him, ironed his clothes, picked him up from the bus stop, taught him his speech, etc.

Andre was twenty when I let him know that I knew for certain about his activities. He said to me, "Mama, I miss my brothers. Things haven't been the same since Chucky died, and now Vincent is in prison for something that he did not do. Mama, I'm going to get this money and that'll be it. I have to bring Vincent home so that we can have our family back. That's all I want."

I said to him, "God won't have us to do it this way."

He heard me, but he wasn't listening. He went right on with his mission to the point that he was almost robbed and had been shot at several times.

By this time, Vincent and I were talking again.

CHAPTER 6

Thou Art the Potter

August 2013 was the final break of my on and off again eight-year relationship. I had gone on another one of those drinking binges. I became very belligerent toward my man while accusing him of draining all of my strength to the point that I had failed my children.

Yes, this was a very horrific blow up, and once again I blacked out. Early Sunday morning, I awoke trying to remember what had taken place the night before. While I was lying still, multiple scenes of what I had displayed began jumping out at me. I couldn't believe what I was hearing myself to have said. I got up, went into the bathroom, and looked in the mirror but couldn't stand to look at myself. I was so ashamed for how bad I had talked to him and for how I had continued to force myself in this unhealthy relationship which had caused me to neglect my children. I had plans of going to Sunday morning service as usual, except this Sunday felt different. I felt so ugly that I got back in my bed, covered my head, and cried myself to sleep. There I stayed all day and night.

The next morning, I saw my son and granddaughter off to school. I spent most of that morning talking and listening to God. I must have apologized to myself at least a hundred times that day as I would gaze in my mind, reflecting back on how I had failed my children over a period of seven years. I had stopped being the active mom when Charles died.

Sure, I was in the house which was no longer a home, I spent money seeing to everyone being fed, sheltered, and clothed, but I had become the passive mom because in all truth, I was just there. Being able to acknowledge and admit my wrong to myself is what led me to have a one-on-one heart-to-heart conversation with each of my children. I started by apologizing for how I had knowingly failed them as their mother. One by one they began telling me how I had hurt them. My eldest child, Katrina, expressed to me how they had all, including Vincent, talked about getting me some help but were afraid of what I might do. With them knowing who I really am and that the person that I had become wasn't me, they didn't want to bring anymore shame on me even though they were ashamed of me. Apologizing to God, my children, and myself took a great load off of me, and I felt like I was on solid ground again. My relationship with God and my faith had become strong once again, and as for my children, we have gotten closer, but there's still healing that must come due to years of hurt.

From that Sunday, I would go almost a year without a drink.

Within that year, Andre would crash into a steel dumpster after being shot.

It was a beautiful Saturday afternoon, around 2:30 p.m. I had just pulled into my driveway, and as I was exiting my car, I heard several shots. I walked toward the back of the house dialing Andre's phone to tell him that they were shooting in the city, so please do not come down, but he never answered. I proceeded in the house, grabbed the broom, and began sweeping my second floor steps when halfway through I heard beating on my front door.

I asked, "Who is it?"

The voice I heard on the other side was very familiar, so I opened the door but not prepared for what I would see and hear. She was soaked in blood and said, "Andre's been shot in his head."

I was sweeping which was the same thing I was doing when I got the knock on the door about Charles. This time I was calm yet concerned.

You see, one late night, Andre was parked in my driveway when I came out of the house. I walked over to him, and he said to me, "Mama, they are trying to kill me."

I looked at him very shocked and said, "Son, you don't tell your mommy—" At the same time that I was saying, "mommy," I shouted, "Yes, you do tell me what is going on so that I can pray with you and for you!"

So you see on that Saturday while she was standing at my front door screaming, I was talking to God in the spirit telling Him how He's made me promises and one of them was that Andre would be kept.

I called my sister Lynette and said, "Andre's been shot in the head, and I need my family."

Within a few minutes, my mom and three of my sisters were at my house. After briefing them on what I had just been told, my sisters and I went into the kitchen, held hands and began to pray while our mother stayed up front interrogating the lady who had brought the information. I called my daughters. They were so distraught that they rushed to my house.

A few minutes after they had made it, my telephone rang, and I heard, "Mama."

I smiled and was praising God all at the same time because it was Andre. When he walked in my door, I ran to him, we hugged, we kissed, and I was telling him how I thank God that I am not at the morgue identifying him. He told me how he thanks God for protecting him and sparing his life.

There was a wide, thick bandage on his forehead and so much blood on his clothes. I can tell you that I know God to be a buffer. He was there in that car, shielding Andre that day just for me.

Less than two months later, Andre would go to jail for eluding the police which led to a high-speed chase causing me to be mad at him but sad because I was separated from another one of my children, and his first child would be born while he was incarcerated.

Andre has made some wise, valuable decisions while being incarcerated.

Today, I am thankful for things being, as well as they are and proud of Andre's maturity.

CHAPTER 7

Could It Be Déjà Vu

A month after Andre was arrested, my oldest brother died. I was sad but relieved that he was no longer in any pain. I felt bad that my sons couldn't be there. My brother was such a great uncle to them, and they looked up to him. My brother was headstrong about what was right. He loved my children and watched them grow from infants to adults. I felt bad that Vincent and Andre couldn't be present, yet I was grateful that I still had my youngest son at my side. My youngest son, Darren has grown into a fine young man despite all of those troubled years with me as his alcoholic mother.

Darren loves his brothers and does everything right to help the both of them and their children. One of the proudest days of my life with Darren was when he graduated from high school two days before my birthday on May 16, 2014. I say this because the first three of his high school years were unsettling due to me not participating in his education like I had done for most of his elementary years even after Charles died.

Even then, he still had Jabria and Andre living at home who were a big help, but by the time he entered high school, they had both moved out. This was the same year that Vincent was sentenced to prison, and those first three years I drowned myself in alcohol. I would fuss at Darren when he would get a bad grade, ask him if he was having problems learning, and tell him that I was coming to the school, but never showed up because I would have started early drinking for the day. There were many times he would try to fix it all by himself, and he would do just enough to keep from hearing my mouth.

The summer of 2013, Darren had to attend summer school. I knew without saying it to him that this was my entire fault, and when I received a notice of where he was to report for school, oh my goodness, I was terrified! All these years, I had kept him away from what I had thought to be outside negativity, and I didn't let him walk to the neighborhood stores by himself in fear that he might become contaminated of the wrong environment.

Although we have always lived in a lively neighborhood, my children didn't go to school with our neighbors. It was never because I thought we were better than anyone, but I've always wanted better for my children and worked hard at it up until I lost Charles. The beginning of Darren's senior year happened to be the same time I stopped drinking. This was wonderful, along with the fact that he had passed the class in summer school.

He had my attention just like it was before Charles died. Not only am I proud of my son, but his two brothers are so proud of him as well.

Sunday, May 18, 2014, was my birthday, and this was a beautiful sunny day. This was the first time in a long time that I was sober and in my right mind on my birthday. I felt fantastic and free. One of my old coworkers, who I also consider as my nephew, had called me right after I left church and said that he was on his way over to pick me up for dinner. The food was delicious. It was a delightful evening. He took pictures of me then he took me to my baby girl's house. There I spent the rest of the evening with her and my grandchildren and took more pictures.

It was now the beginning of summer, Darren had graduated, and my granddaughter was out of school. He decided he would move in with my cousin, who's a sergeant, in order to be closer to work. My granddaughter wanted to move back home with her mother and siblings. Everyone thought that I would get lonely and lose it because I had never been by myself. I grew up in a house full of siblings. I had my first child at the age of sixteen, five more after her, and I always had at least one man hanging around. There was no way that I could manage by myself so they thought. I believe that if I had not gone through the loneliness, which I suffered dearly when Charles died, and the separation from Vincent, I would not have known that feeling. However, I can assure everyone that being alone and being lonely are two different things. For me, one doesn't compare to the other. Alone, yes, and I'm embracing it; I'm enjoying getting to know me the way it was intended from the beginning of time, but as for me being lonely, not for one moment.

My daughter Katrina called me one day and said, "Mama, I was talking to Grandmama, and I told her that I understand her being by herself since Granddaddy died because she's in her seventies, but my mama is in her forties, and I don't know how she can stand being in all that house by herself, and she acts like it doesn't bother her."

I told my big girl, "Baby, mama has never had any time to herself. I've been responsible for six other people right here in this house. I've had to cook when I didn't feel like it, go to work regardless to what it felt like outside, and not only care for myself and take myself to the doctor, but also, all of you. Now here it is no one but me to look after. Don't misunderstand me because in a way I still do look after you but from afar. See, I have set boundaries for myself because after all, you all are adults now with your own families, and it's time that we all take what we've learn collectively and make it work for us individually. No more bigger pots on the stove unless it's the holidays or a special occasion. I'm grateful for all the love that we shared throughout this house and the many memories of my children, and grandchildren. I've already sat back and laughed about some, but this, right here, is so new to me, and I feel like I have gotten my groove back or may I say, 'A groove that I never knew that I had, and nothing, or nobody is going to disturb my unspeakable joy.'"

Her response was, "All right, Sweet Kim."

This is how she would always end our conversations, if it's a good conversation, and she knows that I am adamant about something.

A month later, I accepted a job back in automotive, something I'd really enjoyed in the past. After I had been on my job, not quite two months, God spoke to me in my bedroom. I was standing at the foot of my bed, and He said, "Write."

I, knowing the voice of the Lord, spoke back and said, "Write? You're telling me to write now?"

At that moment, with scenes running through my head about what to write about, I said, "I don't even have a title."

God spoke, "I'll give it to you, you just write."

It wasn't long before God told me that my title was, "*The Story That Must Be Told.*" *Wow*!

I remember that following Sunday, right after morning service, sitting on the front pew talking to my sisters and my mother, I told them that God told me that it was time for me to write. A couple of my sisters knew that I had been trying to write again several times after Chucky died, but nothing would come out, so for me to have this great flow now was a miracle. See, I had written the story of Chucky's death. I started writing it when he was about two years old, and the title of that story was "Where *Will I Spend Eternity?*"

My uncle, who was my pastor at the time, allowed me to put it on as a play at the church on October 31, 1999. Charles died just like I had written it five years later. Here is what I've come to understand: we have all been predestined to something in life, and that everything and everybody has a purpose and season. If you want to accomplish yours at the reasonable, enjoyable time then you must let go of certain people and places that are not relevant for the fulfillment of your destiny.

Spring 2015, I was faced with whether or not I could organize a union for employees who work at a company whose owner has had a good, successful business for more than thirty years. No one had ever attempted this leap. Witnessing how a union was much needed for these loyal people in order to be respected and treated fairly, I made what I believe was a wise decision after much supplication with God to go through with this plan. After the votes were counted, these people won the right to a union. This was one of the happiest days of my life and another great accomplishment. I knew that if they had not won, then the company would possibly dismiss them and God knows, I didn't want this on my heart. I knew that these were dedicated hard workers. They put in so many overtime hours just to meet the fork in the road in order to make another week for their families, so I, knowing how passionate I am for what's right, had to see this through.

CHAPTER 8

The New Beginning

A few months later, my daughter Katrina went through a severe illness causing her to be hospitalized three times in a matter of two months. She was near death once, according to doctors, leaving me to bare much heartache, knowing that her two brothers she talks with daily couldn't be at the hospital with her to see for themselves that she would be all right. Feeling what I was feeling for them was painful for me. On the 25th of September, my baby girl's birthday, I got a phone call from Katrina's neighbor while I was at work. She began frantically telling me that Katrina is having difficulty breathing and that the paramedics were on their way. I'm sure that if her neighbor could, she would tell you, just how irate I was that she couldn't answer my questions. Seemingly, she just happened to stumble upon my daughter outside. When the paramedics arrived, they told the neighbor that Katrina was in distress and that they must get her to the nearest hospital which was approximately two miles from where she lived. I jumped in my car. I was crying and scared, but I was talking to God reminding Him, not that He had forgotten, that my two sons were incarcerated, and that He promised life for my children and me. I knew that my sons would lose it if something happened to their big sister. I must be honest because at that moment, I had a sidebar with God, and I said to Him that my daughter must live, be healthy, and continue being the mother, which included her seeing after her own children, not me as their grandmother.

Before I left work, I called my sister Carol but did not get an answer, so I called my sister Lynette. She answered while visiting at the hospital with our mother, who had to be taken to the hospital by ambulance the week prior. While driving down Highway 70, my baby sister, Aleida, called me and immediately, she and another person began praying for my daughter and me. I began to hear my sister specifically declaring fresh breath inhaling and exhaling in Jesus name.

She told me to do it. She repeated, "Breathe, Kim, inhale and exhale, in Jesus name."

As I did that, I was again talking to God in my spirit about the promises He's made me. Then my other end rang, and the paramedic told me that my daughter was no longer in distress, so they were detouring to Barnes Hospital where the doctors were familiar with her health. Being that she was out of distress and other family members were on their way, I stopped and picked up Darren. Darren moved back home with me the month before this crisis to be close to his now government job.

Once we were at the hospital, I began breaking down after being told that my daughter was back in trauma where my Chucky was when he died in 2004. It was suddenly a déjà vu. I could not go back to see my baby. I asked my son to do the same thing that I had asked his father to do eleven years earlier. Only this time, my son would look at my daughter and tell me if I could handle seeing the condition she was in. When he returned, he said that I could handle it, so we both went back where she was, and I tell you this, I had a fit.

My baby was so swollen, eyes were shut, and she was shivering and was trying to say "Mama." Oh Lord, this was so hard for me. Right at that moment, my sister Sandra entered the room; her eyes were big staring at my daughter. She began praying for Katrina declaring in Jesus name that she will live. I, being overcome with emotions, excused myself, and went in the lobby where other family members were.

An hour later, my phone rang while I'm in the lobby. It was Vincent, and I couldn't bring myself to answer the phone, so I gave it to Sandra. He asked Sandra why was she answering my phone, she tried to tell him what was going on, but he told her that he wanted to speak to me. He began to tell me how he knew something had to be wrong because he had talked to Katrina earlier that morning when she had come in from work. He had tried calling her several times later, but she never answered. Then he asked if I would take the phone to the back and put it to her ear so she could hear his voice. I attempted his request at least four times on two different phones, and each time I came close to reaching her room, we lost reception. This caused me to become very sad for my son.

Katrina did recover, and she went home that same weekend. Although she's given me a couple of scares since that day, I prayed that she'd find her way as I've had to find mine after so many years of my own self-pity. I have had many adversities over these past years and have been at my lowest point were others noticed. For one reason or another, they wouldn't bring to my attention just how low they had seen me fall. One friend of mine told me while we were reminiscing about how low I had fallen that he knew I had hit rock bottom, but he said that there was something in me that although I was down, I never would go under and for that reason, he knew that I would be okay eventually. I thank God that through it all, I have remained solid in my faith, knowing what is revealed about Him in Romans 8:28–29 NKJV. It reads, "And we know that all things work together for good to those who love God to those who are called according to His purpose. For whom He foreknew, He also predestined to be conformed to the image of His Son, that He might be the firstborn among many brethren."

Amen.

Summary

Romans 8:27–39 NKJV:

Now He who searches the hearts knows what the mind of the Spirit is, because He makes intercession for the saints according to the will of God.

And we know that all things work together for good to those who love God, to those who are the called according to His purpose. For whom He foreknew, He also predestined to be conformed to the image of His Son, that He might be the firstborn among many brethren. Moreover whom He predestined, these He also called; whom He called, these He also justified; and whom He justified, these He also glorified.

What then shall we say to these things? If God is for us, who can be against us? He who did not spare His own Son, but delivered Him up for us all, how shall He not with Him also freely give us all things? Who shall bring a charge against God's elect? It is God who justifies. Who is he who condemns? It is Christ who died, and furthermore is also risen, who is even at the right hand of God, who also makes intercession for us. Who shall separate us from the love of Christ? Shall tribulation, or distress, or persecution, or famine, or nakedness, or peril, or sword? As it is written:

> "For Your sake we are killed all day long;
> We are accounted as sheep for the slaughter."

Yet in all these things we are more than conquerors through Him who loved us. For I am persuaded that neither death nor life, nor angels nor principalities nor powers, nor things present nor things to come, nor height nor depth, nor any other created thing, shall be able to separate us from the love of God which is in Christ Jesus our Lord.

Acknowledgments

To my children, I can't say enough how sorry I am for the years we've lost due to the passing of my son, your brother, Chucky, and the injustice, four years later done to my other son, your oldest brother.

Words can *never* express how my heart aches knowing that what once was hasn't been for many years. I pray as we work toward healing one another, we would realize how close we were and that our individual hurt is due to our disconnection. Do know that mommy loves you *always* no matter who or what is in the storm.

My son, Charles Montez Wallace (Chucky), my *all* around guy who left this life too soon, will *always* be loved and have a special place in my heart. (December 03, 1986–May 13, 2004)

My earthly father who has passed from this life, Professor John A. Wallace Sr. will always be the most loving, caring, and gentle giant of *all* times in my eyes.

I love you, Daddy. (January 08, 1930–February 13, 2008)

To my mother, my love, thank you for standing by me throughout my entire life even when I wanted to be a daddy's girl. I'm thankful for how God has brought you through and is allowing you to be kept among us.

I love you, Momma (Dot), and I will forever cherish every precious moment that we shared (April 11, 1940-October 05, 2017).

About the Author

Kimberly Michelle Wallace was born to Mr. and Mrs. J. A. Wallace Sr. in St. Louis, Missouri. At the young age of just sixteen, Kimberly gave birth to her first born. And by the age of thirty-one, she'd birth six children, two daughters and four sons. Kimberly would have her children sit at the kitchen table *every* evening doing homework while she'd cook a full-course meal after working an eight-hour nursing job.

Most nights after dinner, she would read a few Bible scriptures, sing hymns, and pray over her children before letting them go to bed. Kimberly was most proud for the success of her oldest two sons who were both dominating forces in their sports arena. This kept Kim busy most weekends. Kim kept her children very active in church.

In 1999, she purchased her family home. In May of 2000, she married her sons' father. A month after she married, she changed her career becoming an automotive machine operator.

Kimberly's life was pretty normal even with the challenges that came with being a mother to six different personalities, she'd *always* seem to have control.

May 2004 began several years of many hardships for Kimberly.

Today I am persuaded that Kimberly Michelle Wallace has use of many references which will allow her to reach her destiny in greatness.